HUG HELLO, KISS GOODBYE

MANPREET KAUR

Made with ❤ on the Notion Press Platform
www.notionpress.com

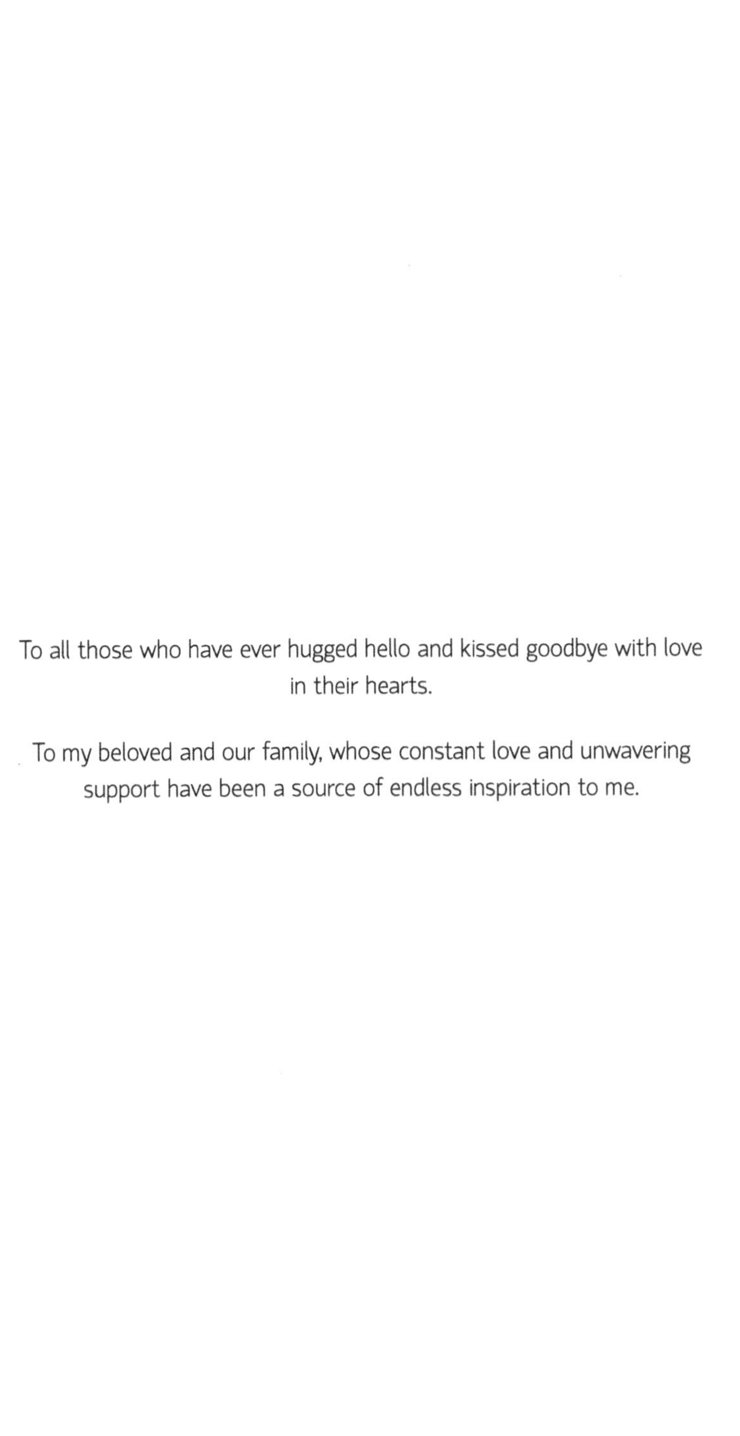

To all those who have ever hugged hello and kissed goodbye with love in their hearts.

To my beloved and our family, whose constant love and unwavering support have been a source of endless inspiration to me.

Contents

Contents

Contents

Contents

Preface

He replied, "Because you have so little faith. Truly I tell you, if you have faith as small as a mustard seed, you can say to this mountain, 'Move from here to there,' and it will move. Nothing will be impossible for you."
(Matthew 17:14-21)

Acknowledgements

This book is a testament to the power of human connection and the emotions that it evokes.

It is a tribute to the love, joy, pain, and longing that we all experience as we navigate through life.

I am deeply grateful to all those who have touched my life in some way,

and whose experiences have inspired me to write this collection of poems.

To my family and friends, thank you for your hugs and kisses that have lifted me up in the darkest of times,

and have inspired me to explore the depths of human emotions through my writing.

To my readers, thank you for joining me on this journey.

I hope that my words have touched your heart and soul,

and have reminded you of the power of a hug hello and a kiss goodbye.

This book is a celebration of life, love, and the beauty of connection.

May it bring comfort, joy, and inspiration to all who read it.

A JOURNEY OF SELF DISCOVERY

May we all be tourists of the cities we live in,
Explorers of the worlds we inhabit,
And astronauts of the galaxies inside ourselves.

UNTANGLING EMOTIONS

How do I feel?

No one has asked me that exact question in a long time. Of course, people ask me how I am, but that is different. It feels like the answers I can give to that question are so limited, and I do not want to break any boundaries that I have established for myself. I am afraid that if I open up to someone, they will feel the constant weight of my responsibility to keep up with how I feel, and I do not want anyone to feel like that. It is easier to be forgotten.

But back to how I feel. I feel lighter on some days, heavier on others. I am talking about the thoughts in my head and the feelings that pass through me. There are emotions I try to avoid, of course, like sadness, loneliness, feeling unworthy or undesirable. But I am human, and the thing that characterizes my humanity the most is my ability to feel and to have an intellect.

Despite my fears, there is a certain closeness I crave that I have not experienced yet. It is a connection that goes beyond just small talk or surface-level conversations. It is a deep, meaningful connection where I can truly be myself and be understood. I long for someone who will listen to me without judgment, who will hold space for me to be vulnerable and open. Someone who will be there for me, no matter what. It is a tall order, I know, but I cannot help but I have always believed that there is someone out there who can fulfill that role in my life.

CHAPTER THREE

CLOSED BOOK

Three years had passed,
Since we said our last goodbyes,
And for me, they were final,
An emphatic full-stop punctuation,
Ending a years-long sentence.
But now you try to edit my ending,
Change the period, line break, chapter break,
Into a semicolon, maybe even a comma,
But I will not let you.
You have no say in this story anymore,
And I will not even dignify this ridiculous request,
With a response- well, not one that you can access.
I have closed the book on our history,
And the ink has long since dried,
No matter what you try to do,
This story is over, and I have turned the page.

CHAPTER FOUR

A WAKING ACHE

I took this ache to bed with me,
And was somehow surprised
When I woke up next to it,
In the morning, bleary-eyed.
It had nestled in my chest,
As I had closed my eyes to rest.
It had lingered in my dreams,
And had followed me to the dawn it seems.
I tried to shake it off,
But it clung on tight to me.
I tried to ignore its weight,
But it was all that I could see.
It seemed to grow with each moment,
Feeding on my fear and doubt.
It seemed to be all-consuming,
Till I felt I could not get out.
But then I remembered,
That pain is a part of life.
It is the price we pay for love,
And the joys that make us thrive.
I took a deep breath and sighed,
As I faced the day anew.
For even though this ache still hurt,

I knew I could make it through.
I stood up tall and faced the sun,
And let its warmth embrace me.
For even though the ache remained,
I knew that I was free.
Free to choose my path ahead,
Free to learn from this ache.
Free to love and live again,
And to all that life may make.

CHAPTER FIVE

CITRINE STARS AND WHISKEY LIPS

On that San Francisco street, the world seemed to fade away, leaving only you and me amidst the misty evening air.

The scent of whiskey lingered on my lips as we shared a cigarette, the smoke swirling around us like a cloak of intimacy.

As we stood there, talking with our coworkers under the glow of citrine stars and the hum of sodium-bulbed street lamps, I felt a nervous excitement bubbling within me.

Every time our fingers brushed against each other, a spark of electricity passed between us, igniting a flame of desire that I could no longer ignore.

In that moment, I knew that I was not going to make it home that night. I was hopelessly drawn to you, caught up in the magic of the moment and the irresistible pull of your presence.

As we walked the streets together, our steps in sync, I felt a sense of belonging that I had never experienced before.

The world around us seemed to blur as we talked, lost in each other's company, our hearts beating in time. And when we finally parted ways, I knew that my life would never be the same.

That night, beneath the citrine stars and the glow of the street lamps, I had found a piece of myself that I had been searching for all along.

CHAPTER SIX

LEARNING TO CLOSE DOORS WITH GRACE

Because I do not know how to close doors
I only know how to slam them.
Perhaps it is time to break the cycle,
To find a way to reconcile,
To mend the bridges that I have burned,
And show the love that I have earned.
So I will start with one small step,
And try to curb my anger's depth,
To close each door with care and grace,
And find a new, more peaceful space.

CHAPTER SEVEN

LIVING FOR LIFE

The feeling was....

It is how people do not die, but they do not live either,

they live, moving towards death, for, most of them live only to die.

But there are those who live to live, who seek the moments that they can give,

to others and to themselves,

to find the joy that life compels.

They feel the sun upon their skin, and revel in the world within,

The colors, sounds, and scents surround,

a life that is lost but can be found.

The feeling that we all seek,

is not the end, but what we keep,

in the moments that we are alive,

The memories that will survive.

For death may come, as it will,

but the life we lived is with us still,

and in our hearts, we carry on,

a legacy of what we have done.

So let us live, and not just be,

a stepping stone to eternity,

for life is precious, life is grand,

and we must live it while we can.

CHAPTER EIGHT

AGONY OF A LOVE LOST TOO SOON

Please I just feel a little too young
to have loved and lost
People say not to rush in too soon
but I would have loved you much sooner
if I knew what it would cost
because losing you before you know how
much I love you
is agony
and that is not something I want to hold onto
for the rest of forever.

CHAPTER NINE

SHATTERED RESOLUTIONS

All around her, the air shimmered with the heat of intoxicated resolutions, soon to be broken, and the tacky residue of ball-drop midnight kisses. The world seemed to spin and blur, like a kaleidoscope of colors and sounds that refused to come into focus. And she felt herself slipping, her emotions as slick as the condensation-covered cheap champagne flute, barely perched in her hand.

She tried to hold on, to cling to some semblance of stability and control, but it was no use. The glass slipped from her fingers, falling to the hardwood floor with a shattering crash. And in that moment, she felt her heart shatter too, as if the sound of the breaking glass was a reflection of her own shattered dreams and hopes.

The echoes of the glass against the wood seemed to reverberate through the early moments of the dawning year, a reminder of all that had been lost and all that was yet to come. She stood there, frozen, unable to move or speak, feeling as if she were trapped in some kind of waking nightmare.

But then, slowly, something shifted within her. A spark of determination, a glimmer of hope. She realized that this was not the end, that there was still time to pick up the pieces and start again. She took a deep breath, letting go of the past, and stepped forward into the new year, ready to face whatever lay ahead with courage and strength.

CHAPTER TEN

IN THE CADENCE OF THE NIGHT

The world is taking on a familiar grey cast,
Darkness approaches, and I find it difficult,
Not to let it crash over me like a wave.
Prone on my bed, eyes closed,
My heartbeat a thrumming bass line,
Echoing within a stuttering rhapsodic melody,
Irregular and unpredictable.
The weight of the day bears down on me,
An unrelenting pressure, a relentless tide,
But still I cling to the rhythm of my own pulse,
Finding solace in the syncopation of my breath.
In the silence of the night, I am not alone,
For in the cadence of my heart and the melody of my
soul,
I find a constant companion, a faithful friend,
Leading me through the dark and into the light once
again.

CHAPTER ELEVEN

DUALITIES WITHIN ME

Always, I have felt torn in two, like a walking set of opposites both attracting and repelling. I am a contradiction, a paradox of emotions and desires that seem to pull me in different directions.

At times, I find myself feeling confident and self-assured, radiating a magnetic energy that draws others towards me. But then, in a sudden shift, I become overwhelmed by self-doubt and anxiety, pushing those same people away.

I am both attractive and repulsive, a dichotomy that I struggle to reconcile. It is as if there are two halves of me constantly vying for dominance, neither one willing to yield.

In conjunction, these opposing forces create a tumultuous inner landscape, where joy and sadness, love and hate, hope and despair, exist in a fragile balance. It is a dizzying and exhausting experience, one that leaves me feeling both exhilarated and drained.

Yet, despite the constant push and pull, the contradictions and conflicts, I have learned to embrace my duality. For it is in this complex interplay of opposing forces that I find my true self, ever-changing and evolving, a beautiful mess of contradictions that make me who I am.

CHAPTER TWELVE

MEMORIES OF A LOST WORLD

Do you remember the days before everything fell apart?
I do,
vividly.

I remember the way the sun would cast golden rays across the sky as it set, the vibrant hues of red and orange that would bleed into the clouds, and the way the air would hum with life.

I remember the bustling city streets, the sound of laughter and music spilling out from bars and cafés. I remember the people, their faces filled with euphoria and expectancy, their hearts filled with oneiric and ubiquitous yearnings.

But now, each night they come to visit me, these memories, of what once used to be, haunts me with their bittersweet embrace and taking me to a time and place, reminding of everything I have lost, the price I paid, the painful cost of what was and what is now lost. There is no relief, no release from these memories that refuse to leave my head.

They are a constant pain, an endless loop of regret and shame. With no relief, no rest in sight, they haunt me through the day and night. Yet still I cling to them, desperate to hold onto something that feels real and alive, something that is not tainted by the darkness that has consumed our world. These memories are a reminder of what we have lost.

THE ROAD NOT TAKEN TOGETHER

There was no road map
No guide
We go lost
We stumbled in the dark
With no stars to light our path
Tripping on our own hearts.
And as we searched for a way out
We took a wrong turn,
And I lost you.

CHAPTER FOURTEEN

ASSYMETRICAL AFFECTION

I realize
I am not
half as
much to you as
you are to me.
You occupy my thoughts,
like the air that I breathe,
but I am just a footnote,
in your life's grand scheme.
I cherish every moment,
with you,
oh so rare,
but to you,
I am disposable,
easily replaced,
I am aware.
Yet still, I hold on tight,
to the fragments of your love,
knowing deep down inside,
I am not enough.

CHAPTER FIFTEEN

A COFFEE SHOP ENCOUNTER

Focus lost
words blur into
background noise
even though she
feels she should
hang on every syllable
the movement of his lips
so full of grace
hypnotizing
alluring
enchanting
all she will remember
from this night
is the curve of his smile
when he laughs
and the way he
sips his coffee
delicate and slow
she has never before
been jealous of a ceramic mug.

CHAPTER SIXTEEN

FADING INTO STRANGERS

"We will never know
each other again."

We once shared everything, our hopes, our dreams, our fears, but now we are strangers passing by, with memories soaked in tears.

We thought we would be forever, two souls intertwined as one, but life took us on different paths, and our love slowly came undone.

Now we stand on opposite sides, of a chasm too wide to cross, we will never know each other again, our love, a beautiful loss.

CHAPTER SEVENTEEN

THE ISSUE IS YOU

The issue is that I did not even pick an outfit yet.

The issue is that I have not saved his number on my phone yet but I still have not brought myself to delete yours.

The issue is that I say I am giving him a proper chance but I still think about you more than I would ever like to admit.

The issue is that I am writing this.

The issue is that you are still the main character in all my poems.

The issue is that he is "him" and you are "you".

The issue is that the playlist I made when I should have been sleeping.

The issue is that I was relieved when I did not feel a connection and was relieved when the stars would not align in his favour.

The issue is that I am holding on, to memories that have long gone, and it is hard to let you fade away, when your presence still lingers every day.

The issue is that I compare, every little thing that we share, to the moments that we had before, when you were still mine, and nothing more.

The issue is that I know, that I need to let you go, but my heart just cannot seem to move on, from the love that we had, and now is gone.

Maybe someday soon, I will see, that you were just a memory, and that I deserve a love that's true, not just a faded shade of you.

CHAPTER EIGHTEEN

FROM STRANGERS TO LOVERS OVER BOURBON

As we sat at the dimly lit bar,
I could not help but feel a sense of camaraderie with you.
We had both come to drown our sorrows and forget our troubles,
and somehow,
in the midst of all that chaos,
we found each other.
As we took turns buying rounds and sharing stories,
I found myself drawn to your laughter and your quick wit.
It was as if we had known each other for years,
even though we had just met.
And as the night wore on,
our conversations became more intimate,
more vulnerable.
And finding common ground in bottom shelf bourbon,

we talked about the things that we had never dared to
share with anyone else,
the things that kept us up at night and the things that
made us feel alive.
And as we shared more of ourselves,
I began to see the person behind the pain,
the light that shone through the darkness.
You were funny,
and kind,
and brave,
and I knew that I had fallen for you.
The night seemed to stretch on forever,
and before I knew it,
the sun was rising and we were stumbling out of the bar,
arm in arm.
I did not want the night to end,
but I knew that I had found something special in you.
Looking back,
I cannot remember exactly how we fell in love,
but I know that it was that night.
The night we drank to forget,
but ended up remembering each other.
And I would not change a thing about it.

DRIVE ON TO DRIVE AWAY

Hope you did not get a
speeding ticket
when you left.

I hope the wind was kind to you, as you drove away, out of view, may the road ahead be smooth and clear, with no speeding tickets to interfere.

I hope the sun shone bright that day, and the music on the radio made you sway, may the memories of us fade away, and bring you peace, not sorrow, as you stray.

I hope you find the love you seek, and all the happiness that you dreamt to keep, may your heart be filled with joy and light, and your days be filled with hope and delight.

But most of all, I hope you know, that even though we had to let go, you will always hold a special place, in my heart, where love will never erase.

BOUND BY SELF DECEPTION

You tied up your own hands
and looked at me with sorry eyes
as if to say "you did your best,
but my hands are tied"
I do not know how to forgive you
for believing your own lies
when you refuse to accept
we could be on the same side.

BOOKISH CONNECTIONS

Sometimes, during my morning commute, I share a fleeting moment with a stranger. He sits across from me, absorbed in one of my favourite books, translated into the language I am learning.

As I steal glances at the pages he turns, I am filled with a sense of wonder and longing. I yearn for the day when I will be brave enough to share a brief bookish moment with him, to connect over the shared love of literature and language. But for now, I remain a silent observer, content to bask in the familiarity of the words that dance across the page. In this moment, I am reminded of the power of books, how they have the ability to transcend language and culture, to bring people together in a shared experience.

As the train lurches forward, I close my eyes and let the rhythmic clack of the tracks lull me into a reverie. I imagine a world where strangers become friends over the pages of a book, where language barriers are broken down by the universal language of storytelling.

And in that moment, I feel a sense of hope, a glimmer of possibility that perhaps, one day, I will summon the courage to share a bookish moment with the stranger across from me.

CHAPTER TWENTY-TWO

REACHING FOR NEW SKIES

You can change as much as you want to,
Or as much as you need to,
And you do not have to apologize for it.
For change is inevitable,
In this journey called life.
It is the only constant,
In a world that is always in strife.
You do not have to hold onto,
What no longer serves you well.
You do not have to carry,
The weight of an old shell.
You can shed your old skin,
And embrace a new you.
You can step into the unknown,
And explore a world that is brand new.
For change is not weakness,
But strength in disguise.
It is the power to grow,
And reach for new skies.
So do not be afraid to change,
Or to let go of the past.

For every new beginning,
Is an opportunity to last.

CHAPTER TWENTY-THREE

FADING FEELINGS

Funny how feelings fade,
A decade ago, if you had told me,
That he would become nothing to me,
Just someone I used to know,
Never would I have believed,
Or dared to hope, that could be true.
Funny how feelings fade,
And the past stops aching,
November no longer tastes like him,
A fate I feared,
when I was young and consumed by angst.
Funny how feelings fade,
The thing I thought I would always want,
Rarely ever crosses my mind anymore,
And I do not miss it, or him.

CHAPTER TWENTY-FOUR

WHAT IS LEFT OF US

In the early morning hours,
I recite my unfinished poems to the empty room,
As if you were standing right in front of me,
listening to each verse,
but the words turn to ash,
and the ash disappears into the air,
leaving me gasping for breath in the emptiness of our shared space.
You apologize,
and yet the burning skies remain dry,
in this part of the town,
forgetting is a luxury we cannot afford,
but I am learning that it is okay to lose parts of ourselves sometimes,
that in the broken pieces of our lives,
beauty can still be found.
Somewhere near the corner store, in a vibrant town,
a sculpture stands tall,
made of different objects in pieces,
a reflection of our own fractured selves,
yet still standing strong,
testament to the fact that it is okay to lose parts of ourselves sometimes.

For in the cracks and the broken pieces,
new light can shine through,
illuminating the path forward and showing us what is
left of us,
a reminder that even in loss,
we can still find beauty and hope,
that the fragments of our lives can be put back together
again.
What is left of us may be different than before,
but we are still here,
still standing,
still finding our way forward.

CHAPTER TWENTY-FIVE

STEPS TOWARDS LOVE

If I showed you
what love can be,
would you take another step
towards me?
If I showed you
the depths of my heart,
And shared with you
every single part,
Would you take my hand
and never depart,
Or would we be doomed
from the start?
So tell me, my love,
what will it be?
Will you take another step
towards me?

BUILT A BRIDGE

At any given moment
during a span of too many years
the distance between
my life as I lived it
and the life I wanted to live
seemed a vast uncrossable chasm
bit by bit
with the assistance of those I love
I built myself a bridge
and now I test our construction
I do not know if it
will hold my weight
and although I am not yet
safely to the other side
this gap no longer intimidates me
there are worse fates
than falling.

CHAPTER TWENTY-SEVEN

THE WEIGHT OF IT ALL

The first month
of this new year
has felt almost infinite
stretched by added responsibilities
paperwork and procrastination
anxiety dreams
short nights
self-inflicted stress
and external forces
but yesterday
how liberating it was
to try new cuisine
with my fellow expats
conversation and laughter
and mangú and cerveza
alleviating my problems
the weight of it all
lifting from my shoulders
and I floated freely home.

CHAPTER TWENTY-EIGHT

APPEALING TEMPTATIONS

The heart yearns for what it cannot have,
and the mind plays tricks in the absence of love,
as we struggle to navigate the treacherous waters,
of desires and needs,
and the longing for another.
But perhaps the true lesson lies in learning,
that we do not need someone to complete us,
that we are already whole on our own,
and that the bad guy is not worth the compromise.
For in the end,
it is not about who wants us,
but about who deserves us,
who respects us,
and who loves us for who we are,
flaws and all,
and that is the one worth fighting for, after all.

CHAPTER TWENTY-NINE

WINTER'S LAST GLIMMER

The day is short
and the breeze holds
winter's crisp bite
but the sun
low in the southern sky
graces us with
warm yellow light
as we stroll exposed
low-tide sandy expanses
searching for seashells
and we breathe in waves
the salty tang of ocean air
as the last day of the year
fades toward its end.

CHAPTER THIRTY

LOVE LIKE THE FULL MOON, LIVE LIKE NEW YORK

You love like the full moon,
Illuminating everything in your path,
Bringing light to the darkest corners,
And warmth to even the coldest hearts.
You live like the New York,
A city that never sleeps,
With energy and vibrancy that never fades,
A place of endless possibility and potential.
And when I look at you,
My heart cracks open like a seed,
Blossoming into a flower of love and adoration,
Nourished by the light and energy you provide.
You are a force of nature,
A marvel of the universe,
And I am humbled and awed,
To be in the presence of such greatness.
So let us dance in the moonlight,
And explore the city that never sleeps,

For together, we can create a love,
That shines as bright as the full moon,
And lasts as long as the city that never fades.

• 42 •

CHAPTER THIRTY-ONE

REACHING FOR STARS

As a child, I gazed up at the top shelf,
reaching for dreams that felt too wild and out of reach,
longing for change, for something beyond the sounds,
yet terrified of leaving these small, stagnant towns.
Staring at the vast expanse of the night sky,
I breathe in deeply, contemplating what I might become,
wondering if I will sell my dreams for something cheap,
if I dare to reach for the stars and find my wings.
But as I inhale the darkness,
I am filled with dread,
fearful that the light will surround me
or leave me for dead,
and I cannot help but wonder if I will one day look back,
and see that I stayed in place, afraid to take the leap.
For life is a cycle, dry and mundane,
full of lost dreamers and their shattered aspirations,
trapped in the cycle of quiet suburban despair,
yearning for something more,
something beyond the glare.
And I never want to look at myself in the mirror,

with a soulless, sad stare, the weight of regret too heavy to bear,

trapped in the endless cycle of a life that is barely begun,

forever yearning for something that I have yet to become.

CHAPTER THIRTY-TWO

JUST OUT OF REACH

You are right there,
But you are also long gone.
A memory that lingers on,
A shadow in my heart at dawn.
I see you in the streets,
In the faces of strangers I meet.
I hear you in the wind,
Whispering secrets of love and sin.
You are a part of me,
But you are also free.
Free to roam the world,
To find your own destiny unfurled.
And though we have said our goodbyes,
And though the tears have long since dried,
I still hold a piece of you,
A memory that will forever be true.
For in loving you,
I learned to love myself,
To embrace the beauty of life,
To find my own wealth.
And though we may be worlds apart,
You will always hold a special place in my heart.

CHAPTER THIRTY-THREE

KALEIDOSCOPE OF BUTTERFLIES

You are my longtime favourite muse,
A fountain of inspiration that never fades,
But I fear to confess the truth,
To risk losing the electric thrill that pervades,
Whenever I receive your words,
A kaleidoscope of butterflies taking flight,
In a symphony of flutters and whirrs,
A blissful sensation that feels just right.

CHAPTER THIRTY-FOUR

BREATHE WITH ME

I will try
not to ask
for too much
At heart, I am an
independent creature,
Proud and self-reliant.
But sometimes,
When life overwhelms,
And I struggle to draw breath,
I might, just maybe,
Request for you to be my lungs,
To help me breathe for a little while.
An hour or an afternoon,
Just long enough to fill me with oxygen,
And remind me how to inhale and exhale.
For even the strongest among us
Need a helping hand sometimes,
A brief respite from the struggle of life.

CHAPTER THIRTY-FIVE

RESTLESS AS THE RAIN

The world stretches vast before my wandering feet, beckoning me onward with a siren's call. Restless as the rain, I roam through forests and fields, across mountains and seas, searching for something that I cannot name.

Each step takes me further from the familiar, deeper into the unknown. I am driven by a hunger that cannot be sated, a thirst that cannot be quenched. I am a wanderer, a nomad, a seeker of truth and beauty.

Through every storm and every sun-kissed day, I press on, driven by an inner fire that cannot be extinguished. I am a part of this world, and it is a part of me. Together, we stretch out endlessly, a canvas waiting to be painted with the colors of life.

And though I may never find what I am searching for, I know that the journey itself is worth the effort. For in every step, every breath, every moment of wonder, I am alive. And that, in the end, is all that truly matters.

CHAPTER THIRTY-SIX

THE WEIGHT OF MISTAKES

Sometimes,
she wishes she could simply delete herself from all her connections-

business,

personal,

and familial.

It seems easier to be lost in the ether, to fade into oblivion, than to face the reality of her own shortcomings and faults.

The weight of her mistakes and failures bears heavily on her mind, causing a gut-wrenching anxiety that she can barely stomach. To simply disappear into the abyss would be a relief, a chance to escape the consequences of her actions and the pain they have caused.

Yet, deep down, she knows that this is not the answer. To run away from her problems would be the ultimate act of selfishness, a refusal to take responsibility for her actions and ask for forgiveness.

Instead, she must face her demons head-on, no matter how difficult or painful the process may be. She must confront the people she has hurt, the bridges she has burned, and seek to make amends.

For only by facing her mistakes and asking for forgiveness can she hope to find true redemption and healing. And though the journey may be long and arduous, she knows that it is the only path worth taking.

CHAPTER THIRTY-SEVEN

GALAXIES IN YOUR EYES

Whenever you happen to slip into my mind, bearing memories of fleeting, occasional hours spent in your comforting presence, my chest aches. It is as if my heart is pumping razor-edged chips of garnet through its chambers, instead of warm liquid blood.

You crystallize me, filling my mind with visions of galaxies hidden within your eyes, and I am overcome with a longing to make a home there, to explore every nook and cranny of your soul.

But then reality sets in, and I am left with the bitter knowledge that we are merely ships passing in the night, two strangers whose paths happened to cross briefly before moving on.

Still, I cling to the memory of you, like a lifeline in the tumultuous sea of life. For though our time together was short-lived, it was a bright spot in an otherwise dark and uncertain world.

And who knows, perhaps our paths will cross again someday, and we will have the chance to explore those hidden galaxies together, to create a new home in the infinite expanse of the universe.

CHAPTER THIRTY-EIGHT

THE EXERCISE OF SCIAMACHY

The daily battle
that reads
like a checklist

- Keep hydrated
- Eat fresh foods
- Get enough sleep
- Exercise
- Write

is an exercise
in sciamachy
my only opponent
is the darkness
that never truly
leaves me alone
often casting
its ugly obscuring shadow
over my otherwise
bright days
but I am well-seasoned

in this lifelong practice
and most days
I defeat
this imaginary opponent
most days
but not all.

CHAPTER THIRTY-NINE

FINDING PEACE IN LOVE'S GOODBYE

In the midst of a bustling city, amidst the honking of cars and the hustle and bustle of people, there stood a couple on the rooftop of a skyscraper. They stood there, lost in each other's eyes, as the city noise faded into the background.

The wind blew gently, ruffling their hair, as they leaned in for a kiss. In that moment, time stood still, and they were the only two people in the world.

As they parted, they knew that their love was fading away, like the echoes of the city sounds that were slowly dying down. Yet, they couldn't let go, for the adrenaline rush of being together, of being lost in the moment, was too strong.

They held each other tightly, as the memories of their time together flooded their minds. The moments of joy and laughter, the times of tears and pain, all of it came rushing back, like a wave that couldn't be stopped.

In the silence that followed, they knew that it was time to say goodbye, to let go of what was once a beautiful love story. Yet, in that moment of stillness, they found a peace that was bittersweet, a moment that they would always cherish.

As they walked away from each other, they knew that their love would remain, like the memories that they had shared. And though they were no longer together, they knew that they would always be a part of each other's story, like the echoes of their love that would never truly fade away.

YOUR ABSENCE

As it turns out, I did not need you at all.
Your absence allowed me the perspective
to find strength and love
in my own presence.
I learned to cherish solitude,
To find comfort in my own skin.
I no longer seek validation,
For my worth comes from within.

EMBRACING THE WONDER YET TO BE

Amidst the hum of steaming brews and clinking cups,
a girl sits lost in thought, her mind ablaze.
A solo traveler, in a land unknown,
with fears and doubts that once were all she has known.
But as she sips her coffee, dark and strong,
she feels a change, a shift within her soul.

For in the past year, she said goodbye to the scared girl who barely lived, just survived.

Now, she has come so far to be right here, this moment, in this coffee shop, alone.

And though doubts and fears still linger near, she chooses to embrace this life, to thrive.

For she is like a bird that has learned to fly, and spread her wings, to seek and to explore.

The world is her oyster, and she has come so far, to this exact location, time, and space.

And as she looks around, she sees anew, the beauty of this city, bright and fair.

For every street, every corner holds the promise of adventure, joy, and hope.

So let her sit, and sip her coffee strong,

for she has come so far, and yet there is more to see.
A traveler, a dreamer, a girl reborn,
ready to embrace the wonders yet to be.

• 58 •

MISSED OPPORTUNITY

Sometimes I wonder
how different our lives
might be now if we
had not been interrupted
that night in my car.
You are my last lingering
what-if from a lifetime
of missed opportunities.

CHAPTER FORTY-THREE

TEXT I DID NOT SEND

The bitter bite of an IPA reminiscent of your lips.

Cigarette smoke wafts memories of late nights outside bars,

in front of your hotel, wasting time talking under starry lights.

You linger with the burn in my throat when I shoot Jameson.

I hope the wind blows you back to me one day.

CHAPTER FORTY-FOUR

YOU GAVE UP TOO SOON

The irony is that I am on a path to live the wild dreams we shared,

But I must do so without you, as fate has declared,

You surrendered too soon, caved into the "real world" paradigm,

While I waited for my moment, my stars to align.

I will send you pictures from the corners we will never explore,

The ones we spoke of with such fervor, but not anymore,

The streets we will never stroll down,

the sunsets we will miss,

The adventures we will never have,

the chances we will dismiss.

CHAPTER FORTY-FIVE

CHATEAU CARDBOARD

Let us ditch out on life
call in sick and not come back
no doctor's note for "sick of this reality".
Drive south until we find out the perfect beach,
in a quaint little town that feels right,
where the waves crash and the seagulls screech,
For me, all that matters is the simplicity,
of a rickety shack, on a beach by the sea,
and we could call it chateau cardboard
in a beachside town
and each other
and maybe a couple cold beers
at the end of a hot summer day
we will live for love, and love every day.

I GAVE UP ON YOU

I drove past your old neighbourhood today.
My stomach did that slow flip thing it always does,
but it does not feel good like it used to.
I think I finally gave up on you.

SWALLOWING THE BITTER PILL

I swallowed the contents
of both my past
and my fears
on a spoonful all at once
like the bittersweet medicine.
I faced them both
with eyes full of tears.
The taste of regret
of pain
of loss.
Filled my mouth like a bitter, bitter cross.
I begged myself to just keep it down,
To face the demons without a frown.
To learn from the past
and face the future with grace,
To hold on to hope
and keep running the race.
For in facing the bitterest of pills,
I have learned to live
to love
and to truly feel.

ONE TOO MANY

I got drunk on life,
Lost in its pleasures and endless strife.
From the vineyards of Bordeaux,
To the beaches of Biarritz, I did go.
The old trick worked on me once again,
And I was happy,
content,
free from pain.
But then I had one too many,
And everything was buzzing,
my mind so heady.
My thoughts became fuzzy,
my feelings precise,
As I wandered through the streets of Paris, so nice.
The Eiffel Tower looming tall and grand,
As I stumbled through the city, taking it all in at hand.
From the Louvre to the Champs-Élysées,
I drank in the sights and sounds, lost in a daze.
And then I learned my lesson from before,
From overindulging, and waking up on the floor.
Life tasted so delicious, like a fine French wine,
But I knew I had to sip gently, and take my time.
I could not afford another hangover from regret,

So I drank moderately, my senses still wet.
From the beaches of Nice to the hills of Provence,
I took in the beauty of France, a lover's romance.
And I knew that every decision carried its own price,
But I was determined to live life with a little spice.
So I drank in the moments, one sip at a time,
From the cafes of Montmartre to the hills of Lyon.
And though life may be intoxicating,
full of its own maze,
I was ready to face it all,
in its sheer,
unbridled ecstasy and blaze.

CHAPTER FORTY-NINE

LEARNING TO LOVE

We wanted to love each other,
But we did not know how.
We stumbled and faltered,
In the dance of love somehow.
We tried to express our feelings,
But the words would not come out.
We fumbled and stuttered,
In our attempts to speak aloud.
We wanted to hold each other,
But we did not know how.
We hesitated and withdrew,
In the embrace of love somehow.
But then we learned to listen,
To the whispers of our hearts.
We opened ourselves up,
To the vulnerability of love's start.
And slowly but surely,
We found our way to love.
We stumbled and faltered,
But we kept rising above.
We learned to express our feelings,
To share our hopes and fears.
We held each other close,

Through the laughter and the tears.
And now we know how to love,
In all its beauty and pain.
For it is the journey that matters,
Not just the destination we gain.

CHAPTER FIFTY

AVENOIR

As a younger woman I was preoccupied with wandering
which of these scenes
that feel so significant in the moment
would truly last
not be lost to the grey vagary of time
So many years spent
filled with melancholy and avenoir
I forgot that uncertainty can be pleasurable
that life must be lived forward
the journey enjoyable
for its own sake
my feet are on the path
chosen by past-me
and I must trust her judgement
her sense of direction
and blindly stumble forward
To receive the surprising gifts
Waiting at each turn.

CHAPTER FIFTY-ONE

MEMORIES IN AN EMPTY ROOM

I walked into your room,
and immediately,
I was surrounded by memories of you.
Every corner,
every item,
every scent,
all reminded me of your presence.
From the early morning light streaming through the window,
to the shirt you wore on the last day we were together,
everything seemed to hold a piece of you.
As I looked around,
I could not help but wish to kiss your temples and feel the warmth of your embrace once again.
In the quiet moments of the morning,
I could hear my sonnets for you singing silently in my heart,
a melody of love and longing.
But then,
as I sat there in silence,
I could hear your voice in my head,

both killing and soothing me at the same time.
The sound of your laughter,
the way you used to say my name,
the words you whispered in my ear late at night,
all of it flooded back to me,
filling me with a sense of both joy and sorrow.
And in that moment,
all I knew was that you were far away from me,
somewhere beyond the reach of our love.
We could not meet each other sometime,
somewhere,
and the thought of that separation was almost too much
to bear.
But still,
I held onto the memory of you,
hoping that someday,
somehow,
we would find a way to be together again.

CHAPTER FIFTY-TWO

THE CANVAS OF POSSIBILITY

Where do we find beginnings?
In the breaking of dawn,
In the first light of morning,
As we rise with the sun.
When do we decide to start over again?
In the depths of despair,
In the moments of quiet reflection,
As we let go of our fear.
With each new day comes a chance
To leave behind what once held us back
To shed the weight of past mistakes
And find the courage to begin again.

CHAPTER FIFTY-THREE

RUNNING AS FUGITIVES

The scene was eerie as we followed strange shadows into pitch dark alleys.

We knew we were not strong enough to fight our battles alone, so together, we ran.

We were terrified of what was behind us, yet even more terrified of what awaited us ahead.

The only sign of beauty in the midst of all this chaos were the yellow petals on the ground.

They were left to be trampled on, a reminder that even the most delicate things in life can be destroyed in an instant.

The city was consumed by smoke, the same smoke that seemed to be suffocating us.

As we ran, we left our faces behind, becoming faceless people with open wounds.

We were fugitives now, trying to find our way home.

We held on to each other, knowing that if we had to go, it had to be together or not at all.

Our hands were clasped tight, our wounds bleeding together, and our souls intertwined.

In this moment, nothing else mattered but us.

We were a reminder that even in the darkest of times, there is still hope.

As we continued to run, we held onto that hope, knowing that one day we would find our way back home.

CHAPTER FIFTY-FOUR

JUMPING INTO LOVE

What does it mean to stand when you have no idea what falling feels like?

To stand is to have courage in the face of the unknown,

to face your fears head-on even when you have no idea what the outcome will be.

Let us hold hands and cross this river of terror together, even if we do so blindfolded.

Let us paint a colorful life together and teach our lips not to tremble when we call it ours.

Let us write our story into existence, c

rafting our own path despite the obstacles in our way.

Let us jump from the ledge and allow our bodies to know how it feels to fly,

even if it means taking a risk and landing heart-first.

Loving you is like jumping off a ledge.

It is extreme and dangerous,

but I do it anyway because the thrill of being with you outweighs the fear of falling.

It is like quenching a thirst with wildfire,

a passionate and all-consuming love that burns bright and fierce.

In this moment, nothing else matters but us.

We hold onto each other,

knowing that together we can conquer anything that comes our way.

And even if we fall,

we will pick ourselves up,

dust ourselves off,

and continue to chase after our dreams with a renewed sense of purpose and determination.

THE HEART'S CONTRADICTIONS

The heart is just a heart, and yet it holds within it a world of emotions and contradictions.

At times, the heart can be overly sentimental, clinging onto memories and feelings that should have long since faded away. It can be as fragile as annealed glass, easily shattered by the slightest touch or word.

Other times, when you slide your palm to your chest, you do not just feel your heartbeat, you hear a voice. It forgets its ability to pump blood for just a moment and screams people's names fifty to ninety-nine times a minute. Each beat a complete cycle of regrets and missed opportunities.

But sometimes the heart is like a fighter, unafraid of taking hits and standing strong in the face of adversity. And yet, at other times, your heart can be clumsy, constantly tripping and falling over itself.

And then there are those moments when your heart is stuck in the arms of last year's September, unable to move forward and still clinging onto what has already passed.

But through it all, the heart remains just a heart, imperfect and flawed yet still capable of immense love and resilience. It is a reminder that we are all human, and that even in our weakest moments, we have the capacity to grow and to heal.

CHAPTER FIFTY-SIX

GUARDED BY METAPHORS

Every word I choose is measured with precision,
crafted to be just vague enough that you do not find
your laughter casually resting between the lines.
I hide your face behind these strange metaphors,
hoping to keep you at arm's length and to conceal the
depth of my emotions.
But even as I speak in riddles and hide my feelings
behind a veil of ambiguity,
my heart still yearns for connection and love.
And deep down,
I know that true intimacy can only be found when we
are willing to be vulnerable and to risk the possibility of
hurt.

TOMMORROWS AND EXCUSES

One of these days, I will finally shed the excuses and realize the endless possibilities that lay ahead of me.

But, for now, there are still so many tomorrows to come, and I am content to sit here and savor the moment.

After all, I have already paid for this drink - might as well enjoy it.

But, as I take another sip, I cannot help but wonder what the future holds.

What adventures will I embark on?

What challenges will I overcome?

And, most importantly, what kind of person will I become?

There is no telling what tomorrow will bring, but one thing is for sure - I am ready to face it head-on.

No more excuses,

no more holding back.

The time for action is now, and I am ready to seize every opportunity that comes my way.

So here is to the future - whatever it may hold.

I raise my glass in anticipation and excitement, knowing that the best is yet to come.

CHAPTER FIFTY-EIGHT

THE FRAGILITY OF TIME

I do not exist in tomorrow;
this is a fact I am certain of, despite my doubts.
Time is a deceiver with its cunning ways,
always leading us to believe that we have a future to look forward to.
But you and I,
we only exist in the fragments of today.
So, do not be hasty with your promises of tomorrow.
I remember when you said,
"I had an amazing time yesterday, see you tomorrow."
But were you not told that tomorrow is never promised?
That we only have the present moment, which slips away faster than we can grasp it?
So, I implore you to slow down, to cherish this moment we have together.
Tell me everything, why do you admire it so much?
And who knows,
maybe in the middle of a sentence,
I might slip into your forever,
and we will exist in the memories we create today.

SLOW MORNINGS

Let this be how we start each day: the shades drawn, no
alarms.
Let it be slow,
with all the time in the world to reach for each other,
to feel the warmth of skin against skin.
We will lay like this deep into the sun,
soaking up its gentle rays until the last time I roll over
you.
I will sit on your bed,
hand on my thigh,
watching you while the coffee brews.
It is in these quiet moments,
before the chaos of the day begins,
that I find solace in the simplicity of our love.
There is no rush,
no urgency,
just a deep and abiding sense of peace.
And as we sit there,
basking in the warmth of the morning sun,
I know that no matter what the day may bring,
we will face it together,
hand in hand.

CHAPTER SIXTY

COMFORT IN CONVERSATIONS

I feel so comfortable with you,
our conversations do not need to start with a "hey",
it can start from the most mundane of things,
yet it will always feel so special,
like a kiss on a snowy night,
unexpected, but oh so magical.

BALANCING ACT

It is funny how everything seems to matter,
even though we are all hanging by the same rope,
just waiting for the bottom to fall out.
We are all walking on a tightrope,
trying to keep our balance in a world that is constantly
shifting beneath our feet.
And yet, we still find reasons to care, to love, to hope.
It is like we are all in on a secret joke, laughing at the
absurdity of it all,
even as we struggle to make sense of it.

CHAPTER SIXTY-TWO

THE SHIFT

Today I woke with a sinking feeling
As if we were drifting apart
Lying beside you, screaming and fighting
In the deafening silence of our hearts
We were becoming so different
But still, we acted the same
Like actors on a stage, reciting lines
In a never-ending game
And then, something inside me broke
A voice screamed "enough" inside my head
I was tired of the pretending, the fighting
So I said fuck it went back to sleep instead
Maybe it was a form of escape
Or maybe, just a moment of peace
A chance to breathe in the darkness
Before the chaos could again increase
But even as I lay there sleeping
I knew deep down inside
That something had shifted, something had changed
And it could not be denied.

CHAPTER SIXTY-THREE

SOLITUDE AND SELF-REFLECTION

I find myself in a sea of noise and people, feeling like a mere spectator in my own life.

There are several kids playing on the half basketball court which amidst the chaos catches my attention.

How they managed to merge the game of basketball and football, I do not know. But they are kids, and they are happy.

Their laughter and carefree spirit fill me with a sense of nostalgia and envy.

They feel like they own the world.

I am not a kid and I am silent.

I know that I do not own the world, I barely live in it.

I watch myself slowly escape from a group of five.

I head out to the place with the mural paintings.

I examine them like a tourist staring at a monument on a foreign land.

I lose myself in the details, forgetting about the world around me for a moment.

I come back and you ask why I always want to be alone?

I say nothing.

Days later, after a small talk about how my hair has grown by some centimeters since we last met, I tell you how I have not stepped foot outside the house for two weeks. You say 'It is okay'.

that it is okay to feel lost sometimes, to need solitude in a world that can be overwhelming.

And for a moment, I feel less alone, less like a stranger in my own life.

I TRUST THE WAVES

On a crumbling edge
I have seen myself standing
whipped with the wind
and tangled in my own heart
screaming
all I have ever felt
into an ocean
knowing none will ever hear.

THE LONELY THIEF

Sometimes loneliness creeps in like a silent thief,
stealing the light and leaving only grief.
Other times it seeps in, like a morning mist,
clings to my clothes and leaves me in its midst.
I feel its weight upon my soul,
a burden that is hard to control.
The dampness and coldness it brings,
a sign that loneliness has taken wing.
I never knew I was lonely until it came,
a haunting feeling that remains the same.
No matter how hard I try to fight,
the loneliness grips me tight.
And so, I am left here, damp and cold,
a sad and lonely story left untold.

CHAPTER SIXTY-SIX

LOVE AS A HEALING FORCE

Go embrace that person.
Till you hear their bones crack.
Not because they are breaking,
but mending back together.
Till you hear their heartbeat slowdown.
Not because they are dying,
but because they are dying for you.
Kiss their eyes.
For there have been a river for too long.
Let them be the sun for once.
Teach them to shine again.

CHAPTER SIXTY-SEVEN

STANDING ALONE, SURROUNDED BY CELEBRATIONS

Fireworks burst above
as I stand alone in the crowd
their cries of awe and cheer
pass through me
I feel it all
vibrating through every hidden part and I think of every
time
I have stood in this exact spot
in different places
and all I have seen are endings
settling down upon me.

A MESSAGE OF FORGIVENESS

If you see him
Tell him I am not mad anymore
And that I do not hate him
I never did
And I do not think I ever could
Now that I am the age he was
When he took advantage of my insecurities
I think I understand
It feels like a game
And if you do not act cold
You will lose
If you see him
Tell him I am trying to learn from his mistakes
And that I hope he has stopped playing
Tell him I hope he is the warm person
I always thought he could be.

CHAPTER SIXTY-NINE

THE CORRIDORS OF THOUGHT

My mind is a hall of echoing sound,
a maze of thoughts that spin around.
A labyrinth of doors, each ajar,
leading to memories both near and far.
The walls are adorned with portraits of past,
and every corner holds a story to last.
There are creaking floorboards and whispers in the air,
the echoes of laughter, and the cries of despair.
The light flickers, casting shadows on the ground,
as I walk through the corridors of lost and found.
I try to navigate through the maze,
but sometimes I am lost in a nostalgic daze.
My mind is a hall, forever changing and complex,
a place where my thoughts and emotions interconnect.
It is a place where I can lose myself and find my way,
a place where I can explore and create every day.

THE SOUNDTRACK
OF MY LIFE

There is that tune again
humming through the speakers.
Do the same songs
remind you of the same things?
I wonder,
what part of your day I am,
If I am in your world when I am not around
like you are in mine.

THE BRIGHTEST STAR IN MY CONSTELLATION

I am blessed with a multitude of reasons to be happy, yet none shine as brightly as you, my love, my forever favorite. Though at times, you seem like a mirage, a mere figment of my imagination, on other days, you are the sun that warms my heart and soul.

You are the brightest star in the constellation of my own small world, the one that illuminates my path when I am lost in the darkness. I may forget birthdays, keys, and names, but I will always remember the moments we shared, every part of you that you chose to reveal.

I am entranced by the euphonious voice that spills out of you, bursting into song when all is quiet around us. The way you move your hands as you speak, conveying emotions that words alone could never do justice. And that fleeting smile of yours, a rare gem that sparkles in my memory.

I recall the antique silver ring you wore, the one you never took off. Engraved inside was a line from your favorite book, a line that spoke volumes about your spirit and soul: "I would rather be happy than dignified." Every time I asked you about it, your voice would tremble as you stared into empty spaces, lost in thought.

You are my favorite story, my love, woven into the fabric of my life in ways that no one else could ever match. Like every great story, there is an end, but I take solace in the fact that our tale will live on in my heart forevermore.

CHAPTER SEVENTY-TWO

SEARCHING FOR FOREVER

Where can I find
A love I do not have to move on from?
A love that is not fleeting,
But enduring and true.
I have searched far and wide,
Through valleys and hills,
But every time I think I have found it,
It slips through my fingers like sand.
I have tasted the sweetness of passion,
But it fades away like a summer breeze.
I have felt the warmth of companionship,
But it cools down like a winter's eve.
Where can I find
A love that is unbreakable,
That lasts through the ages,
And stands the test of time?
Perhaps it is not a place to be found,
But a feeling to be created.
A love that is built on trust,
Respect, and understanding.
A love that is not perfect,

But is perfect for us.
A love that is not stagnant,
But grows and evolves with time.
Where can I find a love
I do not have to move on from?
Maybe, just maybe,
It has been right here all along.

BEYOND THE MASK

Behind the masks we wear lies a world of untold stories,
waiting to be heard with open hearts and curious minds.
Let us peel away the layers of pretense
and embrace the vulnerability that lies within,
for it is in that rawness that we find our true beauty.

THE UNINVITED VISITOR

I am the visitor you never invited,
Yet I linger on, never subsided,
I bring with me bags of worry and fright,
And I knock on your door in the middle of the night.
You try to ignore me, but I will not go away,
I am the anxiety that you feel every day,
I cling to you like a shadow on the wall,
And I haunt your thoughts, making you feel small.
But do not despair, for there is a way,
To conquer me and make me go away,
Face me head-on, and do not let me win,
And soon enough, I will be just a distant din.
So embrace the challenge, do not be afraid,
For the strength to defeat me lies within,
And with every victory, you will grow stronger,
And my hold on you will be no longer.

AUSTRALIAN CHARM

It is the sound of kangaroos and koalas,
Of beaches,
barbecues,
and bonzer brawlers,
And I cannot help but fall,
under its spell,
This Aussie accent,
that I know so well.

DUAL NATURE OF NOSTALGIA

I run from nostalgia as much as I run towards it.

As it is a double-edged sword,

capable of invoking bittersweet emotions that offer a sense of familiarity,

shaping our identities and allowing us to connect with our past

in ways that are both meaningful and profound

while simultaneously reminding us of the transience and impermanence of life.

CHAPTER SEVENTY-SEVEN

DYING TO LIVE, DYING TO LEAVE

It is a strange paradox that even though loss is an inevitable part of life, our bodies never truly get familiarized with it.

The agony of losing someone or something we love can be overwhelming, and it can leave us feeling as though the ground beneath our feet has given way. It is a visceral experience that can make you feel physically weak, sick to your stomach, and utterly helpless.

In moments of grief, we often long to turn back the clock, to go back to a time when things were different, and the pain we feel now was only a distant dream. But grief has a way of making us feel small and vulnerable, like children once again. And yet, somehow, we call grief a gain because it reminds us that we have loved deeply, and that our capacity for love is greater than the pain we feel.

As grief takes hold, it can be a slow and torturous process, spreading like a venom throughout our bodies until it consumes us. It is like a parasite that sucks the life out of us, leaving us feeling drained and empty. And yet, as painful as it may be, grief is a loyal friend. It reminds us that we are alive, that we have loved, and that we have been loved in return. It is a reminder that even though we are dying to live, we are also dying to leave, and that life is precious precisely because it is fleeting.

THE SYMPHONY OF THE COSMOS

In the depths of the cosmos,
A symphony plays on,
A cosmic harmony,
A celestial song.
The stars are the instruments,
Each one with its own sound,
Playing in perfect harmony,
Their notes echoing around.
The planets dance in orbit,
A celestial ballet,
A choreography of gravity,
In a cosmic array.
And as we listen closely,
We can hear the hum,
The hum of the universe,
A cosmic symphony begun.
Science teaches us how,
Each note comes to be,
The fusion of atoms,
In a cosmic chemistry.
But as we contemplate,

This grand symphony,
Our human emotions,
Are stirred so deeply.
For we too are a part,
Of this cosmic dance,
Connected to the stars,
By some mysterious chance.
We feel a sense of wonder,
As we gaze at the sky,
Our hearts beating in time,
To this celestial lullaby.
The symphony of the cosmos,
Is a song that never ends,
A beautiful reminder,
Of the magic that life transcends.

CHAPTER SEVENTY-NINE

FINDING THE WAY BACK

The once clear path that lay before me now seems to have vanished into the thick darkness of the stormy night. I find myself wandering aimlessly, without a sense of direction or purpose. My eyes, weary from the journey, struggle to make out the blurry shapes and shadows that surround me.

As I stumble forward, I am plagued by the nagging thought of what could have been, what would have been, and what should have been. These thoughts swirl around me like the wind and rain, tossing me about with reckless abandon.

In the chaos of the storm, my wishes seem lost, never given the opportunity to take root and grow into dreams, visions, and eventually, realities. Now, all that remains are the memories of what could have been and the regret of not taking action.

With each passing moment, the storm seems to intensify, making it even harder to find my way. The path, once so clear, has become obscured by the torrential downpour and gusting winds. But despite the darkness and uncertainty, I continue to walk, hoping that somehow, someway, I will find my way back to the light.

CHAPTER EIGHTY

TRAVELING WITH MY PEN

In transit, my pen finds its way,
To capture the moments of the day,
The rhythm of the train,
Or the hum of the plane,
Inspires my words to play.
In cafes, I sip my tea,
And let my mind roam free,
Observing the world around,
As inspiration is found,
In the chatter and the coffee's steam.
On a park bench, I sit and write,
Under the warm and gentle light,
Of the sun shining down,
On the people all around,
As I craft a poem with delight.
From city streets to rural lands,
My muse travels with me in my hands,
Pen and paper at the ready,
As I jot down thoughts unsteady,
And create art from everyday strands.
So wherever I may roam,

My pen is my constant home,
And in my poems, you will see,
The different places that have inspired me,
As I journey and freely roam.

CHAPTER EIGHTY-ONE

SOUL WEARY

I always liked stories of people

seeing, noticing the pain and still waiting for me

moving through so we might grow together dipping our roots down deep

so our hands may reach the sky at the same time and like them

because I never felt soft enough to hold never felt I was worth enough to someone to save so I did it for myself over and over

until I found I was standing alone

further away from people than I ever thought I could be and when I cannot sleep

I get caught in these 2 AM thoughts that know are not true

but are speaking too loud for me to shut them out so I sit here in the dark listening to the rain as it comes steady, steady.

Turn on the light and stare at the cupboard wishing that I might open it up

and still find that old tin that held my stash of dreams or rather

the things that let me dream the M that led me to a quieter place and with a kiss upon my temple lowered me into the river to sleep as deep as the dead and on occasion promise to keep me there.

Instead tonight I think of chewing glass splinters catching in my teeth opening me from the inside

and I wonder why I already know how that feels why that feels like my own memory even more than things I did just yesterday.

In the end, I think all I want to say is am soul weary
But soon it will be time to rest.

CHAPTER EIGHTY-TWO

THE THIN ROAD TO HOME

For the unfamiliar faces we called our own.

For the unfamiliar places we called home.

We convinced ourselves that leaving footprints meant possession.

'To have'.

Having what you so desperately need is desperately terrifying.

Tell me,

how can a person surrounded by water die of dehydration?

'To call something holy'.

To call something holy is to keep your hands on your chest and tell yourself,

'do not touch'.

For the days we felt alienated on our own planet.

'To surrender'.

To surrender is to wave light hands like white flags.

For the days we placed our heads in shallow waters to feel at rest.

'Go a little further' you say.

Do you not know that shallow waters are the most cruel?

'To retrogress'.

To retrogress is to move back to your homeland on a road so thin but strong enough to lead you home.

THE CERTAINTY OR UNCERTAINTY

And my mind
is just an endless shriek a wailing
of notes unreachable
while this earthly time counts away
the fragments of my rotting flesh
but I am sure, yes I am sure
that these seconds have now become hours and may yet
turn to years.

RISING ABOVE HATE

People make you hate, your own self
yet they do not find,
any ounce of guilt to offer.
But I will not let their hate, define who I am inside,
I will rise above their words,
and let my true self shine.

THE AIRPORT SCENE 1

Amidst the chaos of the airport scene,
I stand with my luggage,
waiting in between.
Flights delayed, rescheduled, and cancelled and rebooked
Beeped excess baggage, what else is in store?
But it is not just the weight of my bags that I carry along.
I feel the heaviness of my last baggage,
the weight of time,
Moments that passed and those that I wished were mine.
But I push on,
through the chaos and uncertainty,
Hoping for a smoother journey with a little bit of clarity.
As I wait in the lounge, I witness a sight,
A couple in a fierce and bitter fight,
Their love turned sour, their hearts aflame,
A tragedy unfolding, a love in vain.
I pray to never have a love like theirs,
A bond that is broken, beyond repair,
But deep inside, I cannot help but wonder,
What caused their love to go asunder?

Was it a lack of trust or empathy,
Or perhaps an act of treachery?
Maybe it was a simple lack of communication,
Or a love that was built on a shaky foundation.
As I ponder these thoughts,
my heart aches,
For love is a fragile thing,
easily shattered by mistakes.

CHAPTER EIGHTY-SIX

THE AIRPORT SCENE 2

Amidst the clouds I soar, With Hozier's songs on repeat, Coffee lips and wandering eyes, Lost in thoughts so bittersweet.

The world below fades away, As I escape into the sky, Leaving behind my worries, And all the reasons I can't try.

I take a moment to rest, To pause and just be, Letting my thoughts spill onto paper, Setting my soul free.

Up here, all is quiet, All is still and serene, As if the world has paused, To give me room to dream.

And as I gaze out into the void, With nothing but white in sight, I realize that sometimes, The most beautiful things hide in plain sight.

So I close my eyes and breathe, And let my heart take flight, For up here amongst the clouds, I find the strength to fight.

MIDNIGHT AND MARIGOLD

She wove a crown of marigolds
rested it on her braided locks
and waited for him at midnight
under the old hollow oak
still beating the carved markings
of young love
but the candles she had lit
all the bargains and pleas
she had tried to make
with powers beyond her grasp
meant nothing
as night faded to morning
and the flowers began to wilt
she began to accept
his spirit had already moved on
and she would never get to
hear him say goodbye.

CHAPTER EIGHTY-EIGHT

SOMETHING THAT HAPPENED

Now you are just something that happened to me,
A memory of what once was, but will never be.
Just a passing thought, a forgotten souvenir.
For even though you are no longer here,
You will always be a part of my story, my dear.

CHAPTER 16

We are endless chronicles of possibilities.
A gallery of captured memories.
Memories especially beautiful and especially evocative.
Memories that rarely fade.
Cherished ones and those we bury so deep.
An embodiment of all life's surprises.
Chapters of stories untold.
Stories dying to be told.
Chapter 16;
He picks a pen and a notepad
He fills the world with words so true.
He writes;
We are unending chronicles of limitless possibilities.

CHAPTER NINETY

LOVE ACROSS OCEANS

Across the oceans,
I have roamed,
In search of love,
I have left my home,
To distant lands,
my heart has flown,
And with each lover,
my soul has grown.

TRUTH OR DARE

You hold my hand tightly as if you think I will leave any moment from now.

You look at me, eyes blazing like burning stars.

"I dare you to love me with every piece of you"

YOU and I,

two burning stars.

The article says: "Sometimes stars will collide slowly which results in two stars merging into one. But sometimes the result is a kilonova.

So tell me the truth.

Which one?

CHAPTER NINETY-TWO

LOVE BEYOND RULES

Would you still hug me hello if I kiss you goodbye?
Would you still kiss me goodbye if I hugged you hello?
Can we break free from conventions,
And embrace each other with affection,
Regardless of what others say,
And let our love guide the way?
Can we express ourselves without fear,
And show our feelings loud and clear,
Even if it is not what is expected,
And our actions may be rejected?
Can we redefine what is normal,
And create a world that is more informal,
Where hugs and kisses have no rules,
And love is free to be expressed by fools?
So would you still hug me hello if I kiss you goodbye,
And would you still kiss me goodbye if I hug you hello,
Or will we let society dictate,
And hide our love behind a mask, fake?

www.ingramcontent.com/pod-product-compliance
Lightning Source LLC
Chambersburg PA
CBHW031735150726
47989CB00006B/2474